UNDERSTANDING
COMPUTER NETWORKS

Matt Anniss

raintree
a Capstone company — publishers for children

Raintree is an imprint of Capstone Global Library Limited, a company incorporated in England and Wales having its registered office at 7 Pilgrim Street, London, EC4V 6LB – Registered company number: 6695582

www.raintreepublishers.co.uk
myorders@raintreepublishers.co.uk

Edited by Linda Staniford and Chris Harbo
Designed by Richard Parker and Tim Bond
Original illustrations © Capstone Global Library 2015
Illustrated by Nigel Dobbyn (Beehive Illustration)
Picture research by Jo Miller
Production by Victoria Fitzgerald
Originated by Capstone Global Library Ltd
Printed and bound in China by CTPS

ISBN 978 1 406 28975 6
18 17 16 15 14
10 9 8 7 6 5 4 3 2 1

British Library Cataloguing in Publication Data
A full catalogue record for this book is available from the British Library.

Acknowledgements
We would like to thank the following for permission to reproduce photographs:

Alamy: ©ZUMA Press, Inc., 5; Dreamstime: ©Hobojohn, 30, ©Seanyu, 26; Getty Images: The Image Bank/Peter Dazeley, 28 middle, The Image Bank/David Malan, 18, The Image Bank/Jamie Grill, 14; iStockphoto: ©danishkhan, 8, 43 bottom left, Imagebroker/© hadynyah, 12 left, ©Mark Bowden, 4, ©video1, 34; Shutterstock: Blend Images, 28 left, bloomua, 28 right, 43 middle left, CroMary, 40, Fifian Iromi, 20, michaeljung, 12 right, kurhan, 38, Monkey Business Images, 32, 36, 43 bottom right, Pressmaster, 16, 43 top left, Ferenc Szelepcsenyi, 22, Viktoria Kazakova, cover; Superstock: imagebroker/Jochen Tack, 10, 43 top right.

Design Elements: Shutterstock: HunThomas, vectorlib.com (throughout)

We would like to thank Andrew Connell for his invaluable help in the preparation of this book.

Every effort has been made to contact copyright holders of material reproduced in this book. Any omissions will be rectified in subsequent printings if notice is given to the publisher.

All the internet addresses (URLs) given in this book were valid at the time of going to press. However, due to the dynamic nature of the internet, some addresses may have changed, or sites may have changed or ceased to exist since publication. While the author and publisher regret any inconvenience this may cause readers, no responsibility for any such changes can be accepted by either the author or the publisher.

CONTENTS

Some words are shown in bold, **like this**. You can find out what they mean by looking in the glossary.

INTRODUCTION: WHAT ARE NETWORKS?

▲Computer networks make working, sharing, keeping in touch and having fun so much easier!

Wherever we are in the world, and whatever our age, computer networks touch every aspect of our day-to-day lives. Networks allow us to keep in touch with friends and family, share our favourite photos and videos, work together, have fun, buy things, organize our lives and learn new things.

Welcome to the future…now!

It wasn't so long ago that computer networks were a rarity. Until the **internet** boom of the 1990s and 2000s, networks were much less common. They were expensive to set up and mainly used by universities, governments and big businesses.

Now that has changed dramatically. Today, computer networks are all around us. When you print a piece of homework before handing it in, you're using a computer network. When you use the computer in your school library to help find a book, you're using a network. Many of the fun things you enjoy doing, such as emailing friends, chatting **online** and playing games, are made possible by computer networks.

Join the network

Because they're all around us, we take computer networks for granted. Have you ever wondered how they work, what different types of networks are used for, or what other amazing things we can do with them?

Did you know?

A computer network is two or more computers or electronic devices connected together by cables (wires) or invisible waves of energy (**wireless**). Computer networks are created to let the devices share electronic **information**, called **data**, and hardware such as printers.

CHAPTER 1: HOW DO COMPUTER NETWORKS WORK?

▲The postal service is one of the oldest networks in the world. Its system for collecting and delivering mail uses the same principle as today's computer networks.

Before you can get to grips with computer networks, it's useful to understand exactly what a network is. While today's high-tech computer networks are really complicated, the idea of networks connecting people and places together is not a new one.

Network nation

Networks connect things together, whether they are people, places, homes, towns, countries or continents. Networks of different types bring gas, water and electricity to our homes, let us speak to people on the telephone and send letters and parcels to each other. Then there's the system of roads, railways, tracks and cycle paths criss-crossing the country, which is sometimes referred to as the "transport network". These are just some of the many networks that we rely on every day.

High-tech networks

Computer networks work to the same principles as other "real world" networks. Computers and other electronic devices are connected together, using either cables (what we call wired networks) or wireless technology (what's known as **wi-fi**). Once connected, the computers can effectively "talk" to each other. They do this by following rules, known as **protocols**, which allow them to send and receive data. Once a computer network has been set up, we can use it to send, receive and share data in all sorts of formats, such as photographs, video clips and **emails**.

Did you know?

Historians have found evidence that soldiers were used to deliver letters to far-flung parts of the Roman Empire about 2,000 years ago! This is one of the first recorded examples of a basic delivery network.

Wired networks

Most computer networks around the world are wired. This means that each device in the network is joined together by cables. Data is sent between devices in a network using these wires and cables.

Big or small

Wired networks can vary in size enormously, from two devices (for example a computer and a smartphone), to hundreds or even thousands of computers spread over a wide area. If you have a computer at home connected by a cable to a printer, then you've got your own wired network.

▶Wired networks connect a number of computers and electronic devices together using a system of wires and cables.

Did you know?

Computers in wired networks send data by turning it into electrical signals (or, in the case of **fibre-optic cables**, light), which then travel down cables to their destination. The computer at the other end of the cable then turns those signals back into data.

Computer chain

Simple wired networks usually link computers together in a chain using **Ethernet** cables. These are cables designed to quickly transfer data between computers. Other electronic devices can be added to the network using different types of cables, such as **USB** and **FireWire**.

Some bigger networks use a special type of computer called a **server** to allow many computers to be connected at the same time. There are lots of different types of servers, but all are designed to do just one or two jobs, such as storing documents or connecting the network to the internet.

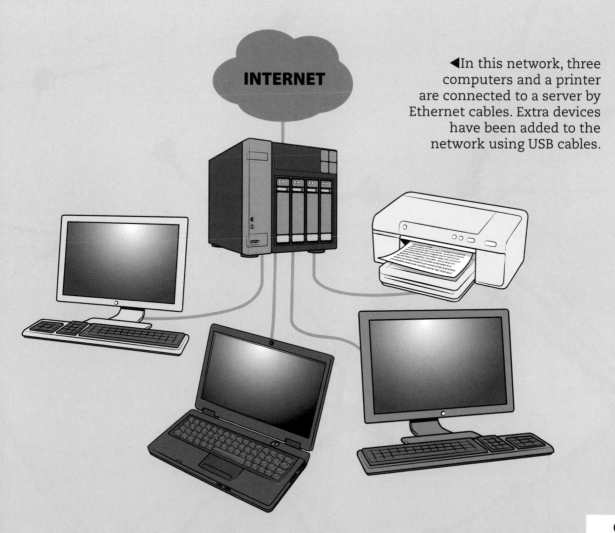

◄In this network, three computers and a printer are connected to a server by Ethernet cables. Extra devices have been added to the network using USB cables.

Wireless networks

◄The same wireless technology used by computer networks is also used in the handheld games controllers that respond to our every move.

Nowadays, many computers and electronic devices don't need to be plugged into cables to talk to each other. Thanks to wireless technology, they can send and receive data through the air.

Wi-fi world

You've probably heard of wi-fi. You may even use it yourself. Wi-fi is a system that allows devices to be connected to computer networks such as the internet without the need for wires or cables. Wi-fi is one of the wireless systems used by mobile phones, laptops and tablet computers to connect to the internet.

Wi-fi-enabled devices use **radio waves**, rather than electrical signals, to send and receive data. The way they do this is amazing…

How wi-fi works

You've just finished your homework on your laptop, and want to print it out on your parents' printer, which can receive documents using wi-fi.

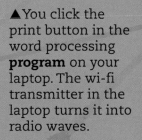

▲You click the print button in the word processing **program** on your laptop. The wi-fi transmitter in the laptop turns it into radio waves.

▲The transmitter then sends these radio waves out into the air. They make their way across the room towards the printer.

▲The wi-fi receiver in the printer detects the radio waves sent out by the laptop. It then turns them back into data and prints your homework.

Did you know?

All wireless networks use radio waves, rather than electrical signals, to send data over long distances. Radio waves are invisible waves of energy that can travel enormous distances. Radio waves are not as reliable for sending data as cables, which is why mobile phone calls often break up and the picture on satellite television channels sometimes cuts out during periods of bad weather.

CHAPTER 2: WHAT DIFFERENT TYPES OF COMPUTER NETWORKS ARE THERE?

▲Computer networks in our homes are connected to much larger networks around the world, allowing us to chat online with friends in different countries.

Computer networks come in many different styles and sizes. Some exist in a single room, house or building, while others span towns, cities, countries and even continents. Each style of network has been designed to fulfill a specific purpose, from organizing our own **files** to working with people on the other side of the world.

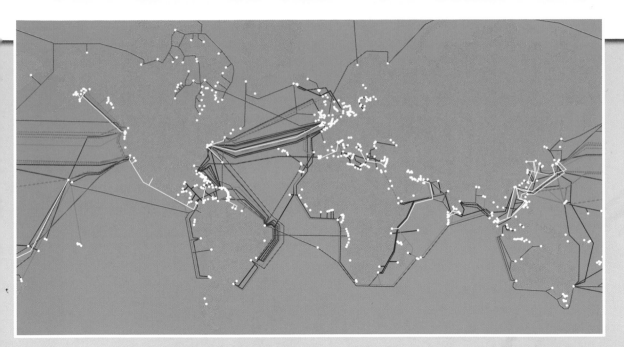

▲Computer networks are joined together by a vast global network of undersea cables, called submarine cables. In total there are over 21,000 miles of fibre optic submarine cables below the world's oceans. They're capable of carrying computer data from one side of the planet to the other in fractions of a second.

We're all connected

Some computer networks exist in isolation, meaning that they're not connected to other networks or the world at large. Most computer networks, though, form part of a much larger network spanning the globe. For example, the computer in your classroom may be connected to a network in your school, which is in turn connected to a network of all of the schools in your area.

The connections don't stop there, either. These networks are your gateway to the internet, which joins together huge numbers of networks and individual computers all over the planet.

Did you know?

Two different types of cables are used to connect computer networks around the world together: telephone wires, which carry data in the form of electrical signals, and fibre optic cables, which send and receive data in the form of pulses of light.

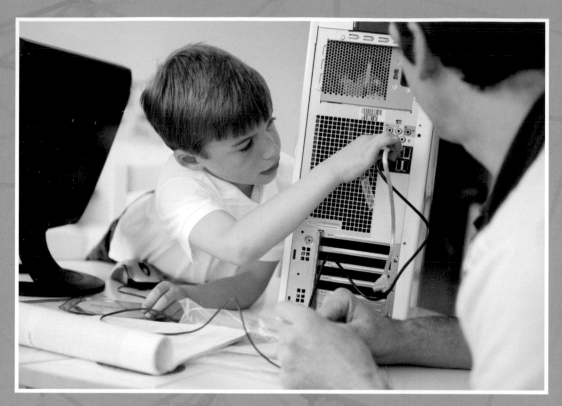

▲If you plug any kind of device into your computer, you've created your own miniature network

Personal area networks

The most basic type of computer network is the one that exists around us. By that, we mean the connections that enable our own electronic devices, such as computers, printers, mobile phones and MP3 players to communicate with each other.

Create your own network

If you've got a computer at home, and any other device that connects to it (either using cables or wirelessly), then you've got your own miniature computer network. That means that if your computer is connected to a printer, or you plug your smartphone into it to transfer songs and videos, you've created a network.

COMPUTER FUTURE

Many personal devices now feature sync features. These use wi-fi networks to automatically transfer important personal data, such as diary entries, photos, songs and phone numbers, between your computer, phone and tablet.

Up close and personal

This kind of network is known as a Personal Area Network (PAN), or sometimes Home Area Network (HAN). Millions of people around the world interact with their own Personal Area Network every day.

▼Your own personal network!

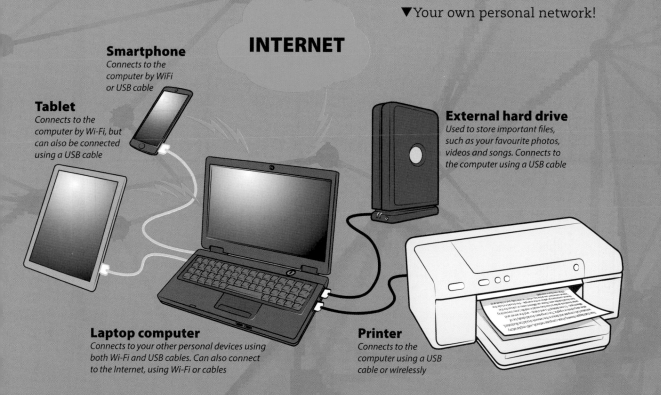

INTERNET

Smartphone
Connects to the computer by WiFi or USB cable

Tablet
Connects to the computer by Wi-Fi, but can also be connected using a USB cable

External hard drive
Used to store important files, such as your favourite photos, videos and songs. Connects to the computer using a USB cable

Laptop computer
Connects to your other personal devices using both Wi-Fi and USB cables. Can also connect to the Internet, using Wi-Fi or cables

Printer
Connects to the computer using a USB cable or wirelessly

Local Area Network

The distinctive feature of a Personal Area Network is that it usually contains just one computer, to which all the other devices connect. If you wanted to connect together a number of computers in your home or school, you would need to set up a Local Area Network (LAN).

▲Local Area Networks allow loads of computers in the same room or building to exchange data and access the internet.

Did you know?

Ethernet cables were invented in 1976 to allow speedy connections between computers in a Local Area Network. They work by breaking down large amounts of data into tiny blocks, called frames. These frames move between computers on the LAN in a fraction of a second.

LANs everywhere

Local Area Networks are very common. In homes, they're used to allow a number of computers to share resources, such as an internet connection and printer. Elsewhere, companies, universities and colleges use them to give employees and students access to important documents, which may be stored on a central **file server** (a powerful computer designed for storing large amounts of data). In most cases, the computers on these larger Local Area Networks also share a single connection to the internet.

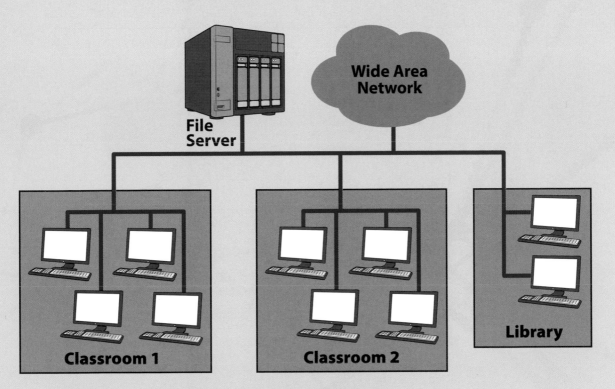

▲This illustration shows how the Local Area Network in a small school might be organized. There are 10 computers in total, with four in each classroom and two in the library. They can all access the file server, which stores important documents such as homework assignments, **information** on coursework subjects, and test papers. The computers also share a joint connection to a Wide Area Network, which in turn connects them to the internet.

Wide Area Network

If we only used Local Area Networks to move data around, the world would feel a much smaller place. We'd be able to connect together computers in one building or university campus, but that's it.

▲Wide Area Networks make it possible to communicate with friends and family all around the world.

Did you know?

Wide Area Networks come in two forms. Some are closed, meaning access is only granted to certain people, such as employees of a company or government officials. Others are open, meaning that they can be accessed by anyone on earth. The world's biggest open WAN is the internet.

Wide, wide world

If you connect two or more Local Area Networks together, you've got yourself a Wide Area Network (WAN). It's a bit like a transport system for data. Think of your Local Area Network as a collection of side streets, the kind that you might live on. A Wide Area Network is like the main roads that join these side streets together, allowing free movement of data around a wider area.

More than one WAN

There are hundreds of thousands of Wide Area Networks in the world. Some are the size of villages, while others stretch around the world. This is possible because data can be sent between LANs by using the telephone lines and fibre optic cables that zig-zag around the globe.

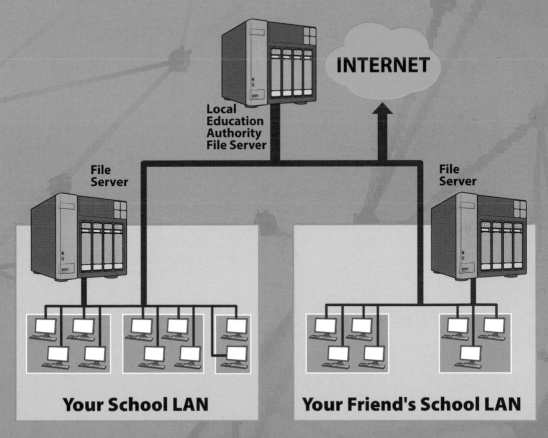

▲This is an example of a WAN that may be used by schools in your town, with each school's LAN connected to the other and to a central file server storing important documents.

CHAPTER 3: WHAT IS THE INTERNET?

So far, we have talked a lot about the internet. But what exactly is it? Put simply, it's a worldwide system of interconnected computer networks. It is possible for any individual computer connected to these networks to exchange data with any other computer on the network, wherever it is in the world. "Internet" is short for "international network".

▶Thanks to wi-fi technology and portable computers, we can now connect to the internet wherever we are in the world.

Did you know?

According to estimates from network experts Internet World Stats, 2.4 billion people around the world use the internet. That's around 34% of the population of Earth!

The host with the most

Every computer connected to the internet is called a host. The user of each host computer can decide which of the internet's many features to access, and what data to make available to other host computers. Any computer can access the internet if it is connected to a Wide Area Network. This is usually done by using telephone lines or fibre optic cables, meaning you can get online even if you're not connected to a Local Area Network.

Did you know?

Like all networks, computers connected to the internet send and receive data by following a set of rules, called protocols. The system of protocols used by computers connected to the Internet is TCP/IP, short for Transmission Control Protocol/Internet Protocol.

Many uses

When we think of the internet, we usually think of the **World Wide Web**. The web is just one of many uses of the internet. Others include sending and receiving messages (email), exchanging data (file sharing) and broadcasting (streaming video and audio).

The World Wide Web

The most significant development made possible by the internet is the World Wide Web. You may have used the web, or at least seen it in action. It's a vast global network of specially formatted documents, called **websites**, which can be accessed from any internet-connected device on the planet.

Web of wonder

Websites are brilliant. They're created in a special computer programming language called HTML (short for hypertext markup language) and can feature any mixture of text (words), pictures, sounds, videos and animations. Websites can be fun, serious, interesting, useful or pointless.

▶The World Wide Web puts all the information in the world at your fingertips. You can find an entire library's worth of facts at the click of a mouse!

Get on the Web

You need to know about the World Wide Web, because it is one of the wonders of the modern age. It's great for finding things out, buying stuff, playing games and even watching funny videos!

Did you know?

The World Wide Web is so big that nobody knows exactly how many websites it contains. Experts believe there are between 600 million and 1.2 billion websites, made up of around 20 billion individual web pages!

A TO Z OF THE WEB

Taking the mystery out of the World Wide Web...

● **Web address:** Every site on the World Wide Web has its own address. This address is used so that people can find it quickly

● **Web browser:** Computer program designed for accessing and reading web sites

● **Web page:** Any single document on the World Wide Web

● **Web site:** Collection of web pages accessed through a single web address

▲Once you're on the World Wide Web, there's an almost endless number of cool websites for you to explore!

How to use the World Wide Web

One of the best things about the World Wide Web is just how easy it is to use. All you need is an internet connection and a simple computer program called a web browser. There's probably already a web browser on your computer or mobile device.

Browse the web

If you fancy checking out a website, the first thing you'll need to do is open up your computer's web browser. Once you've done this, a new "browser window" will be opened. It should look something like this…

`http://www`

This is the address bar. This is where the address of the website you're reading (for example www.britannica.com) is displayed. You can access any website by writing its address into this space and pressing the "return" key.

Web Search

Search

If you want to find something on the World Wide Web, you can search for it. Type a word or phrase into the "search box" and press "return" to search the World Wide Web. Within seconds, your web browser will display a list of websites about that subject.

What's On?
Events in your area.

Weather
Five day forecast.

TV and Radio
Listings for the next seven days

These are shortcuts to other web pages known as "links". Click on one and your browser will go to that page.

This is a video. Click on the arrow symbol to play it.

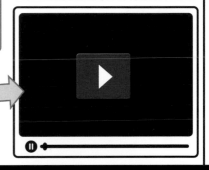

DO'S AND DON'TS

Although there are lots of fantastically fun and useful websites around, there are also plenty of dodgy and dangerous ones. It's not safe to access the web on your own, so ask an adult to help.

Closed networks

◀Closed networks such as intranets are used to restrict access to important data, such as company reports and government files.

The internet is the world's largest open Wide Area Network. However, there are also loads of Wide Area Networks that are not open to the public, they are closed. These are called **intranets**.

Restricted sharing

Intranets are used by big organizations, such as schools, companies and universities, to allow easy sharing of important documents and resources. For example, your school may have its own intranet which you can use to access resources to help you complete assignments or projects, such as encyclopedias and notes from your teachers. Everyone in the school can access these documents, but nobody outside the school can.

Did you know?

Computers on intranets send and receive data in the same way as computers on the internet. However, access to intranets is limited just to people who have been given special permission to use them.

Getting past the firewall

To access an intranet of any sort, you need to get past something called a firewall. This is a piece of **software** that stops people who don't have permission from accessing the intranet.

People with access to the intranet are given their own username and **password**, so that the firewall knows to let them through. These have to be entered to log in to the intranet.

The firewall checks every username and password. If it recognizes it, you're given access to the intranet.

But if it doesn't, access is denied.

CHAPTER 4: HOW CAN I CONTACT OTHER PEOPLE ONLINE?

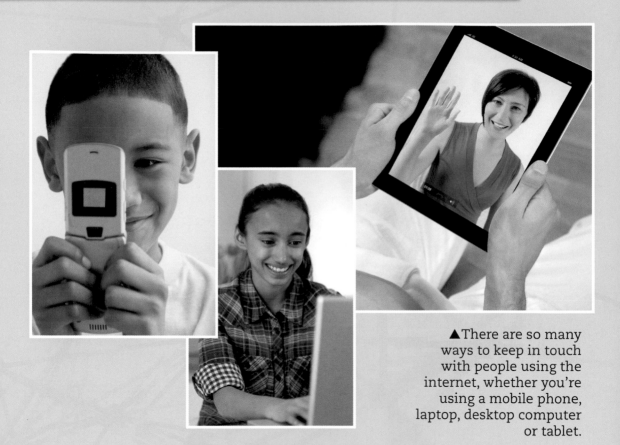

▲There are so many ways to keep in touch with people using the internet, whether you're using a mobile phone, laptop, desktop computer or tablet.

The internet has changed our lives in so many ways since it first began to take off in the late 1990s. The World Wide Web puts a world of information and entertainment at our fingertips, while file sharing allows us to exchange data in the form of files with people living on the other side of the planet.

Snail mail

Arguably the greatest way the internet has changed our lives is the way it allows us to contact other people, and even collaborate with them. In the old days, getting in touch with friends and family far away was much harder. We could send a letter and wait days, weeks or even months for a reply, or we could call them on the telephone, though this was expensive and could be difficult due to the time difference and poor connections.

Always in touch

Things are totally different today. Thanks to the internet, there are loads of different ways to keep in touch with friends, family and classmates. We can send them electronic letters (emails), have a conversation in real time using online chat services, and message them on **social networks**. We can even make video calls to them, often free of charge. Amazingly, we don't have to be sat at a computer to do it – we can keep in touch over the internet using mobile devices such as smartphones and tablets.

Did you know?

The world's first email was sent way back in 1971 by a computer science researcher called Ray Tomlinson. The message, sent over the US military network ARPANET, consisted of just a few random letters.

▲Instead of being posted through a letterbox, email is delivered to computers and mobile devices.

Using email

It's estimated that over 144 billion emails are sent around the world every single day. Email, short for electronic mail, is now the most popular method of keeping in touch with people.

Did you know?

If one of your friends sends you an email, it will appear in the "inbox" of your email program. Any emails waiting to be sent can be found in the "outbox", while copies of sent emails are stored in the "sent" folder.

You've got mail!

Emails are like virtual letters, and they can be sent in a fraction of the time it would take to write and post a real letter. They can be sent and received using an email software program on your computer, smartphone or tablet, or by logging into a web email service such as Gmail or Hotmail.

If you're going to use email, you need your own email address. Everyone who uses email has one. Once you've got an email address, people can send you emails, and you can send emails to other people – as long as you know what their email address is, of course!

Email essentials

▼Here is an email I've written to one of my friends but not yet sent.

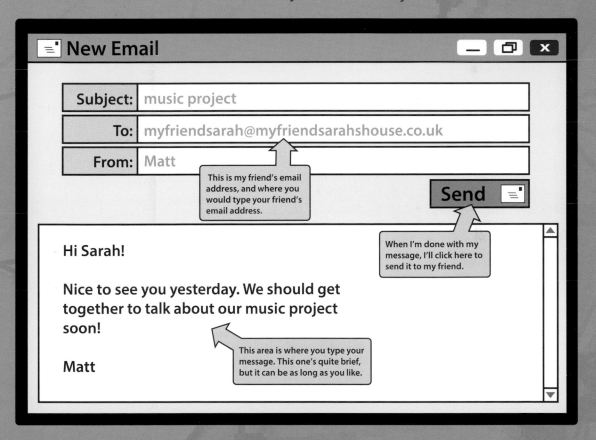

Using social networks

Billions of people now use social networks to keep in touch with friends and family, share photos and videos, and tell the world what they're up to. So what are they, and how can you make use of them?

Be social

Internet social networks like Facebook, Twitter, Tumblr and Google+ are websites that allow users to interact with friends in real time. Once users have joined the network by logging in, they can post short updates about what they're doing, share photos, videos and links to interesting websites, and send private messages to other users.

▲Social networks let you tell the world about the things you love. They are a great way to keep in touch with friends and family.

DO'S AND DON'TS

Be careful when using social networks. Don't accept friend requests from people you don't know, and change your privacy settings so that only your friends can check your photos and status updates. Remember that all of your friends will be able to see what you have written, and it will stay there for a long time unless you delete it! So think carefully about what you choose to share on social networks.

Stay in touch

If your friends are logged into the social network at the same time as you, it's possible to chat to them in real time. It's this aspect of social networks that makes them so useful for keeping in touch with people. If you spot a friend online, you can drop them a message to arrange to meet up, talk about homework or simply hangout.

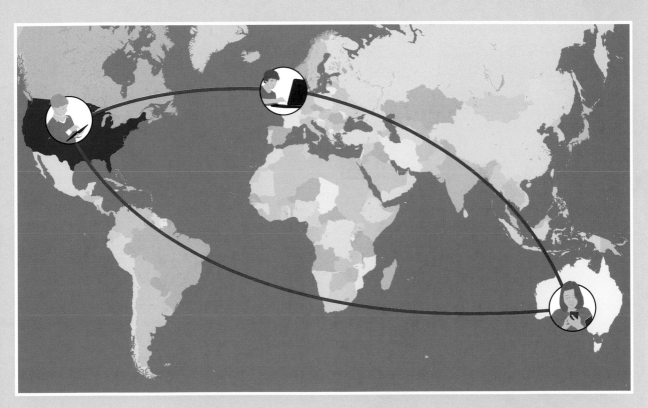

▲The group messaging feature on social networks, for example Facebook, lets you send messages to several friends at the same time, wherever they are in the world. That means if they're logged into the network, they'll get your message within fractions of a second of you sending it.

Using online chat

Online chat, or instant messaging, is one of the most popular features of the internet. Like the "chat" features on social networks, it allows people to quickly send and receive short text messages to other computer users.

▲If you have a microphone and webcam, you can make video calls to friends using programs such as Skype and Google Hangout.

Did you know?

To use online chat services, you'll need an instant messaging program on your computer or mobile device. Many computers now come with these programs built in (MSN on PCs, iMessage on Apple devices). They're very easy to use and don't take long to set up.

How instant messaging works

1 One user opens up their instant messaging program and logs into the system. The user is now connected to the server (known as the client in computer speak) hosting the messaging service. The server responds by sending back a list of other users who are also connected.

2 The first user chooses another user to talk to, and types out a quick message.

3 Their instant messaging program makes a direct connection with the other user's computer. Their message is displayed in the other user's instant messaging program. When they respond, their reply is sent straight to the first user's computer.

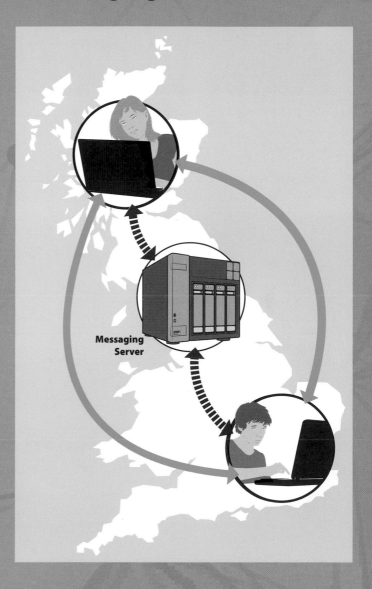

Messaging Server

Using video online

Even more remarkably, some chat services now allow you to see your friends while you talk to them online. All you need is a microphone (which many computers now have built in) and a **webcam**. This is a tiny video camera, designed for use with online chat services – your computer, tablet or smartphone may even have a webcam built in.

CHAPTER 5: HOW CAN I USE COMPUTER NETWORKS TO WORK WITH OTHERS?

▲You're probably used to sitting around a table with friends when you work on school projects together. Thanks to computer networks, you no longer need to do this to work together - you could chat online, send files to each other using email, and even practise presentations using video chat services such as streaming, all from the comfort of your home!

Computer networks don't just allow us to surf the web, watch funny videos and keep track of what our friends are doing. They also open up great opportunities for collaboration. That means joining forces with other people to do cool and useful things, whether that's working on school projects, making music or organizing football matches.

Useful stuff

Once you've got the hang of the World Wide Web, instant messaging, social networks and email, you'll soon realize just how much they can change the way you live your life. Suddenly, instead of phoning friends, you'll contact them online. You'll start keeping track of what you're up to using the diary and calendar programs built into computers, smartphones and tablets. Email will become second nature, and you'll spend some of your spare time chatting to your friends on social media and instant messaging services.

New opportunities

The more you understand about networks, and particularly the internet, the more you'll see how it can be useful when you need to work with other people. You can arrange meetings with your friends by emailing them, discuss school projects using the group video chat feature on programs such as Skype and Google Hangout, and share important documents using file transfer services. Thanks to computer networks, working together is a doddle!

Did you know?

According to official statistics, an amazing 1.2 billion people around the world use social network Facebook at least once a month. That's around one in every six people on Earth!

◄Gone are the days of using a parcels service to move documents around – now you can move the same documents at the click of a mouse!

Sharing things

Computer networks make it really easy to share things with other people. Whether you're using a Local Area Network (such as the one at your school) or the internet, sending and receiving important files can be done with a few quick clicks of a mouse.

Instant transfer

The process of moving files between computers is called transferring. Files can be transferred between computers directly, stored on shared file servers, or be **uploaded** on to file transfer websites.

Did you know?

When you take a file on your computer and transfer it to a website or file server, you upload it. When you retrieve a file from a website or server and place it on your computer, you **download** it.

Ways to share

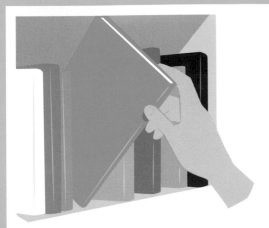

Shared folders
You can share files with other people on your Local Area Network using shared folders. These are like virtual boxes where users of a network can store important documents.

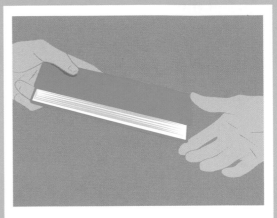

Peer-to-peer networks
Peer-to-peer networks directly connect thousands of computers around the world. Users can upload to, and download from, any other computer on the network, without having to connect to a server.

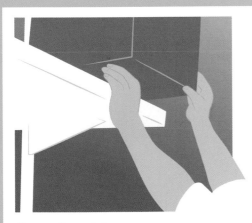

File transfer websites
These websites allow you to upload your files to a storage computer called a file server. You are provided with a link to the location of that file, which your friends can use to download it.

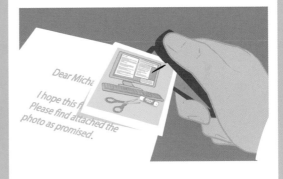

Email attachments
You can share files with people over email. All you do is attach the file you want to send, usually by clicking on a button and selecting the document.

Making blogs and websites

Another great way to work with others using computer networks is to create your very own **blogs** and websites. It's fun, easy to do and they can be about anything you want!

▶ Today, creating your own website can be as simple as making something fabulous from plastic bricks.

Did you know?

A blog, short for weblog, is a simple, diary-style website that can be updated quickly using any internet-connected device. To update a blog, you simply log into it using a password and username, write what you like, and click on the "post" button. Easy! More than one person can contribute to a blog, too, meaning you could invite your friends to help with yours.

Web master

Making websites might seem complicated, but there are lots of website creator services, such as Wix, Wordpress (more famous for blogs, but also allows you to make fully-fledged websites), Moonfruit and Yola, which make the process really easy. You just pick a username (sometimes simply your email address) and a top-secret password, log in to the online website builder, and off you go!

Using online website building services is easy. You simply choose a design, add your own words and photos, and publish it. It really is as simple as that. Why not get together with a friend to make your own site about your shared interests?

DO'S AND DON'TS

We've talked a lot about usernames and passwords in this book. It's important to keep them secret, though it's a good idea to share them with your parents in case you forget them! Passwords help keep your personal details and important files safe from falling into the wrong hands.

CONCLUSION: THE WORLD AT YOUR FINGERTIPS!

Computer networks power the world we live in today. They allow us to quickly send and receive information in seconds, let us keep in touch with friends and family, and find things out with a few clicks of a mouse. Thanks to wireless technology and the internet, we can do all of these things on the go, too, almost anywhere in the world.

Get excited!

If you understand how computer networks work, and what you can do with them, there's no end to the things they can help you accomplish. Want to know when your local sports club is open? Get on the World Wide Web and find out! Need to send some photos to a classmate for your joint project? Attach them to an email and click 'send'.

Just do it!

That's just the beginning of what you can do thanks to computer networks. You could create a website or blog about your favourite band or sports team, have a live video chat with your cousin in Australia, or play networked games against people in Germany, Japan and Jerusalem. Computer networks make communicating and collaborating easier then ever before. So what are you waiting for? Isn't it time you got connected?

DO'S AND DON'TS

Don't forget to stay safe online. Just as you wouldn't speak to strangers in the street, don't chat to people you don't know online. Keep passwords safe, only accept friend requests on social networks from people you know, and if in any doubt, ask an adult to help.

Computer networks straddle the world, allowing us to communicate, send and receive data, and have loads of fun in the process!

GLOSSARY

blog short for weblog. A type of website that can be updated quickly. Blogs are the quickest way of publishing writing on the World Wide Web.

data facts that have not been processed or organised

download process of transferring something from the internet onto your personal computer or smartphone

email electronic mail. Written messages sent and received using computers and smartphones.

Ethernet type of cable used for connecting together, or "networking", computers

fibre-optic cable type of cable made up of many long, thin strands of plastic or glass. So-called because information sent down the cables is turned into pulses of light, rather than traditional electric signals.

file document containing data. Types of files include photographs, video clips, MP3 songs, spreadsheets and word processing documents.

file server powerful computer used for storing data in the form of files

Firewire type of network cable used for transferring data between computers and accessories such as external storage units. Firewire allows users to move data around more quickly than other similar cables, such as USB.

information data that has been organised so that it is useful

internet network of smaller computer networks that join together to form a single global network

intranet computer network that can only be accessed by a small number of people, rather than the whole world

online connected to a network, including the internet

password secret combination of letters and numbers which is unique to one user of a network, website or email service

program application on a computer designed to help you carry out a specific task, for example sending emails, accessing websites and transferring files between computers. Sometimes also called software.

protocols rules

radio wave invisible wave of energy that can pass through the air. All sorts of information can be transmitted using radio waves (computer data, sound, pictures, etc.).

server powerful computer designed for a specific task, for example storing information or running a network

social network website or mobile application that allows users to quickly connect with friends and family over the internet

software computer application or program designed to do a specific task, for example send email (Outlook), edit photos (Photoshop) or record music (GarageBand)

upload the process of transferring something from your computer to a website or file server

USB Universal Serial Bus; a system for connecting electronic equipment to a computer

webcam small video camera that connects to your computer and allows you to send and receive video messages, or record short films on your computer

website collection of writing, pictures, music and sound that is stored on a computer and made available to all on the internet

wi-fi system that allows computers and mobile phones to connect to computer networks without a traditional system of cables

wireless technology that allows the exchange of information but does not require traditional cables or wires

World Wide Web worldwide network of websites

FIND OUT MORE

Books

Careers in Network Engineering Robert Grayson
    (Rosen Classroom, 2011)

High-Tech Science – How Does A Network Work? Matt Anniss
    (Gareth Stevens Classroom, 2014)

How It Works – Telephone & The Internet James Nixon
    (Franklin Watts, 2009)

How The Internet Works Preston Gralla (Que Publishing, 2006)

Oxford Illustrated Computer Dictionary Ian Dicks
    (Oxford University Press, 2006)

Websites

www.thebiginternetmuseum.com
Find out all about the history of the internet with this online museum.
Read about all sorts of weird and wonderful things that have made the
World Wide Web what it is today, from email to peer-to-peer networks
via Skype, Google and YouTube.

http://kids.britannica.com
Stuck with your homework or don't understand computer jargon?
Britannica will have the answers!

www.kidrex.org
Find whatever you need to know on the World Wide Web with this
children's search engine. Just type in a few words, click on the search
button and wait for the results!

http://kidswebsitecreator.com
Creating your own website has never been easier thanks to this simple online site building service.

Places to visit

National Media Museum
Little Horton Lane, Bradford, West Yorkshire, UK
www.nationalmediamuseum.org.uk

This museum is dedicated to all things media related, from radio and television to photography and the internet. It includes a great exhibition on how the internet touches our lives.

The National Museum of Computing
Bletchley Park, Milton Keynes, UK
www.tnmoc.org

Everything you ever wanted to know about computers, from the very first mechanical devices to today's global networks. It also features a working example of the computer that helped the Allies win the Second World War, known as Colossus!

INDEX